The Guest Room of the Heart

Michelle Rau

The Guest Room of the Heart

Manufactured in the United States of America
First Edition/First Printing

ISBN: 978-0-9832405-0-1

Praise for The Guest Room of the Heart

Michelle has pushed aside the stuff of her life to make room for visitors. Polite guests, we drink coffee on the newly bricked porch and listen and wait. Knowing they can now be heard, spirits of everyday things line up to chatter. Spoons rumble about order. A button says, "open me." The faucet drips contempt. A mesquite shakes leaves into our cups. A lizard spouts haiku. And the vine on the porch wants credit for holding everything together. Only the downy comforter in the guestroom offers rest.
—Brandie Erisman, Writer, Reviewer, and Literary Partner-in-Crime

A poet can play with us—tease—entice us to follow where she wants us to go. She can remain partially hidden and still feel satisfied when she puts down her pen. Michelle, however, is a generous poet, cajoling yet delivering verse that is clear and complete. It's a pleasure to read and this first collection is sure to be well-received.
—Marilyn Pincus, Author and Ghostwriter, Arizona, USA

Why

I breathe into his mouth
& make him real

This last stanza from Erica Jong's "Man Under the Bed" has for
years been my mental shortcut to the idea of bringing spirit to life in
the physical world. Now you hold the results in your hand, or in your
eReader.

I enjoyed writing what's in this slim volume, and I grew as a person
and as a writer in the process. It's uneven in quality. I don't care.
Seeing my work published—made real—inspires me to write more.
That's enough for me.

If you're amused or entertained or titillated by anything in these
pages, I'm even happier.

Thank you.

Brody, Brandie, Joan, Deb, Jan, Anne, Stephanie, Erlina, Lonn,
Karen, John, Stephanie, Gene, Michael, Tuesday, Mary, Chris, John,
David, Alison, Sue, Ann, Anne, and Rebecca.

Table of Contents

life

open for breakfast

somebody has to get the day going:
contractors with their pickups full of tools,
two cups of coffee

to flip the sun's breaker switch,
to open the valve that starts time flowing.

we are our own caffeine.
we are the drive to make, do, fix and act.
we are the spark, the ignition.

under our hands darkness brightens,
motors purr into life,
doors unlock
and we're open for business.

dawn

this is why i am a morning person.
they say that dawn breaks
but it really just dawns
like any other realization.

first there's darkness,
but it's not complete.
we can't tell when it becomes light
so we have to listen
and watch for cues.
the birds usually figure it out first,
witness those crazy pre-dawn roosters
and all that.

then a cloud lightens and brightens,
the delicate yellow and pink of potential.
but it still isn't light yet,
we have to wait for the blue sky
to make it official.

or maybe we don't.
maybe it's just a cloudy day
and we have to wait and trust
that the sun will be there
because it is.

the big predator in the sky

dogs get wiggy when it storms—
clinging lurking whining hiding trembling—
when it's their job to protect us.
what's the fuss?

i think there's a big predator in the sky
whose rumbling growls menace and presage
the blinding flash of slashing claws
and tearing teeth.

when your enemy is as large as the sky
and can't be grabbed by the scruff of the neck,
to suddenly find yourself prey
and get pissed on in a most undignified manner,
that just tears it.

the big predator in the sky
electrifies our nerves
and dogs have more hairs
on the backs of their necks.
it must have opposable thumbs;
how else could it fire those gunshots?

you can keep your place
in the food chain, dog,
and i'll take mine
under the fresh driving rain.

harsh mistress

there aren't any new clichés
that can be said about the sea,
but i'll tell you why she's a harsh mistress.

she scours with salt,
abrades with sand,
corrodes with absolute power.

she distorts driftwood and rounds rocks,
tosses seaweed to shore with contempt.
trees grow in strange shapes to avoid her,
and her salty wet perfume pervades every place.

all this before she ever reaches the ships
and before mermaids,
her earthly representatives,
enchant the human race.

her tides can't be managed like menses
or placated like PMS.
paper might cover rock,
but it's soaked by the sea,
and water always wins.

the sea's always on top,
outlasting every marriage
and breaking every human contract.

i can only breathe in the sea,
she makes me exhale in another direction,
turning my breath to her own ends.

she lets me think her pearls of wisdom are my own,
so i'll take her on my tongue every time.

tidepool

a snapshot in time,
one moment between
the sea's flooding of the senses
and the rushing loss of retreat.

it could be a tiny inland lake
but for the sand's inconstant
and shifting boundary.

this starfish looks real,
but beware the barnacles beneath
the slippery seaweed.

take a good look.
the water reflects you now,
as much a part of the ocean as it ever was,
and sooner or later time rejoins the tides.

learn what you can
like a child on a field trip
then send your mirror back to the sea.

j'éclate

like and unlike venus,
i emerge, adult,
from currents.
i spring forth fully formed from my own forehead.

i have always peeled bandaids off slowly;
now there's no time, not even to heal.
scars follow.

trees fell in the forest and i did not hear.
fallen leaves nourished the soil, regardless. now
i am a redwood thrusting forth, thick and fast,
from my own seed.

realizations dawned while i was in the dark.
embers glowed but did not rouse. now
i am a conflagration springing
from my own spark.

cocoon slumber soft as silk
but strong as steel.
wings shed shells, shattering.
nests ignite, implode;
sticks splinter;
fibers shred.

a tsunami surging from a splash.
a concerto bursting from a chord.
a storm thundering from a raindrop.

myself, emerging from myself.

visual feast

i stocked the fridge,
but no one told me
i had to stock the walls
or i would starve.

white space is full of potential
but it's not filling.

now i imbibe with my iris
these shades, shapes and shadows.
now i eat with my eyes
and feast on these frames.
i dine on these designs,
i lunch on these lines,
i can taste this texture.

i gorge on this green,
i drown in this brown.
my gut growls for gold.
i'm yearning for yellow.
i'm ravenous for red.

you, artist.
you didn't know your greeting card
would be the last thing i see every night.
nourishing my dreams
is a huge responsibility.
i want to know that you washed your mind
before you prepared my spiritual repast.

you, photographer.
you didn't know your mountain at sunrise
would be the first thing my lover sees every morning.
he needs a healthy breakfast.
i want to know that you saw god
when you pressed the shutter.

we are what we eat.
we eat with our eyes.
make sure what you serve
will energize.

you sure?

are you sure you don't want
some shiny blonde,
twinkling and sparkling
like a strand of christmas lights,
bright and cold as an LED,
illumination without ignition.

are you sure you don't want
some rare redhead,
a thick full stereotype
whose skin traced between freckles
is cool and smooth as porcelain.
you'll surely find a tempest in that teapot.

are you sure you don't want
some common brunette
from her walnut tresses
to her oak table legs.
it's wood that fuels fire.
stack her thighs on your lap
and strike a match.

conversations, part i

no i haven't been drinking.
no i'm not stoned.
it's true you've never seen me speechless before,
or naked;
that doesn't mean that speechless never happens.

some lines can't be recited aloud;
our bodies don't speak english.
with this much tension,
you can't trust this comfortable silence.
with these premature meanings,
you doubt a pregnant pause.

i wish to defy scientific explanation
and dredge diatoms from silt
without a ripple on the surface. for now.
when the bubble bursts, you'll hear it.

if you don't already know
what my knee is saying to your hand,
perhaps you don't need to know.

thanks for the spackle

it's no accident;
spackle
fixed the holes in my soul,
caulk
filled the cracks in my composure.
sandpaper
smoothed out my own rough edges.

it's no coincidence.
they're an extinct species here
in this old house in north america.
tools were left in my bed;
what's been left in my walls?
someone must have missed a nail hole
where Spirit shines through.

it's no coincidence
that the drywall's worst
in the bedroom
and the closets are too small
for their own doors.
no wall is long enough
for a bed this large;
the ceiling should be twice as high
to hold this much light.

paint hides a multitude of sins
and this room might take three coats.
it's bad feng shui
to hang a mirror in your bedroom
but it's good feng shui
to hang one in your heart.

sonnet for low tide

i walk barefoot, calves creaking,
along a trailing line of dirty foam.
even the hermit crab's not home,
ocean's bounty dead and reeking.

sand dollars speared by gulls, greedy.
barnacles close their shutters tight.
footprints decay in sand and fading light.
retreating waves leave thirsty spirit needy.

no glass floats arrive, no crystal ball
to say which falsely rising wave
will bring the salt and water i so crave.
which of these laps? 'twill be the last of all,

this to be the one that turns the tide,
this to bring the sea back to my soul, inside.

lilith & eve

well, when i was with him, he never

                honey, you don't know the half of it

can you believe that he

                do you remember how he

he used to do this thing, you know

                who died and made him god?

did you ever notice that

                he did what?

but you never wanted kids, did you

                did you ever

so have you heard from him?

                but you two were such a good match

did he ever try

                you let him get away with that shit?

remember that little mole

                he never pulled that on me

does he still have that

                no, i'm wearing it now

carving out time

i carve my life out of free time,
and carve free time into my life.
a chip, a moment,
each tiny stroke texture
in a bland and featureless existence.

watching the sun rise over coffee,
wiggling my toes,
pretending to be asleep,
taking the scenic route home:
these are the tools
with which i sculpt my days.

give me an unstructured afternoon,
a giant slab of time
as solid and pure as marble.
i will find the opening in it.

say no to a life assembled in pieces;
glue weakens wood.
mine will be a continuous whole,
every chance a choice
about what to take away
and what to leave behind,
to bring forth
what's already there.

blesser

blesser (French) *Verb, transitive (a) to injure, wound; (fig) to hurt*

Past Imperfect: je blessais, tu blessais, il/elle blessait, nous blessions, vous blessiez, ils/elles blessaient
Present: je blesse, tu blesses, il/elle blesse, nous blessons, vous blessez, ils/elles blessent
Future: je blesserai, tu blesseras, il/elle blessera, nous blesserons, vous blesserez, ils/elles blesseront

blessure (noun, feminine): injury, wound

in french the word is blessure meaning wound
which is very confusing
because it looks so much like blessing in english
and those of us
who have sustained such blessures
would not call them blessings.

but lucifer was an angel
before his fall from grace,
and every blessure opens the door
to healing, compassion,
to the kindness of strangers.

no matter where the wound
blessures always strike the heart.
they open us to each other;
that doesn't happen often these days.
it's a sad excuse for kindness
but if that's all i get i'll take it.

blesser (verb, transitive): to injure, wound or hurt

j'ai blessé (i have injured)
tu blesses (you injure)
nous blesserons (we will injure)
so now it's up to all of us
to turn our blessures
back into blessings.

checking me out

part of the point of looking better
is having people look.

now i'm a reluctant mirror
for their failings and struggles,
an artificial yardstick
that can't measure their success.

you'd think they're checking me out,
running their gazes over my thighs
and encircling my waist with their wishes,
but the desire i'm inciting
is not for me.

it's for themselves,
or for something they can't yet speak.
i'm held responsible
for reflecting it back to them.

they can choose inspiration over frustration;
i choose the red dress over the black.

i know they notice
when my stocking seams aren't straight,
but the only face i see in the mirror
is mine.

mesquite

you old matriarch,
presiding over the yard
like some demented dowager—
strands flying,
electric in all directions.

you need a haircut.
i'll help you.
it grows back.

fear not, the bees still dote on you,
your annual lovers
buzzing endearments into your leaves
and burying their noses
in your sweet new scent.

birds return, tiny realtors
checking out the condos
and branch offices.
this is a good neighborhood for kids.

you grew tall and gangly like a teenager
on too much soda.
now you've leafed out beautifully.
i'll try to trim you
as carefully as a bonsai,
but would you take a chainsaw to one?
i think not.

eggs

it's 10 pm
and i don't know where my children are
because i don't have any.

one must have slipped away
down the toilet,
another must have snuck off
to the landfill on a pad.

they could be anywhere by now,
long since returned to the elements
or to the elementals
in some cosmic karmic cycle.

perhaps i will pass a child
on the street someday
and there will be a molecule of me
inside of her
and neither of us will know it.

i was born with all the eggs i will ever have.
all the children that could ever be from me
are not.

i'll still hold their potential for them
in my purse
the way mothers always do.

henry's job

it's henry's job
to slow me down,
to make space in time
for words to slip through, key by key.

it's henry's job
to stay my hand
from a frantic dash to the end result
and lead me slow stroke by slow stroke.

it's henry's job
to disconnect me from that grid
and back again to the ley lines of earth;
all the electricity
a girl could ever want or need.

it's henry's job
to shape raw materials of earth
with purpose and intent
into a machine as musical and perfect as any song,
and make me sing it with my fingers.

it's henry's job
to turn mustiness into perfect perfume,
ink into holy wine,
paper into prayer.

the space available

now she can expand
to fill the space available,
the size of an old house
on a city lot
or maybe just the square inch of branch
upon which
the morning's hummingbird sits.

the county assessor doesn't know about
the space available
but it always holds
a raven and a writing desk.

the space available
doesn't hold
does-the-dog-need-her-shots-this-year
or the jesus-that's-overgrown
or the i-haven't-started-my-taxes-yet.

first she rakes the far corners
of the space available:
turns over the soil,
stacks bricks, steps
to an invisible second story
where morning sun
warms a cat, or coffee, or both.

she fills any space available.
celebration, ritual and company
fill any space left in her heart.

proem #1

this is the last of the afternoon sun. but that's okay because this is my last cigarette, which i don't inhale anyway. my dollar store ashtray is imperfect in two ways. nothing so utilitarian need be perfect, i say. it's going to get dinged up some day, frayed in the fray. like this chair, edges decayed, from too many days in this, the last of the afternoon sun.

proem #2

a leaf falls in my glass. i drink it, it's small. how much can a little fly drink, after all? it's clean, maybe a little dust. it's not much. we eat several pounds of dirt a year, so don't fear. this tree is so tall, it can't help where leaves fall. so have some balls and drink your dirt, it don't hurt. sit on your ass, fill your glass, drink more tree, it's free. another leaf falls.

proem #3

each time i go there, there is a new chair. one table becomes two, four chairs eight, maybe twelve if i wait. the couch is leather, unmoving as ever; but the patio table follows the sun, a shiny one. more clothes are lit by a bedside lamp. there's a rack for the clothes that are damp. now there's a third rug where the clothes are hung. the rack is missing a rung. this tablecloth likes the placemats though they're not of the same thread. the third rug is red. the walls are empty, not because of the landlord; they reflect empty space, so no one is bored. did i mention the chairs.

on the vine

they're easy and sweet,
these ones on the end,
they ripen first and fall into the hand.
i'm guilty of seeking rewards without risks,
pleasure without consequences.

after awhile we learn
that bigger isn't always better,
and red doesn't always mean ready.

take a risk, and some snippers.
walk past the field
that smells of mint and miracles
to the the river
that smells of fish and fox.
clear your own path to wild abundance
without the dust of the day.

you'll pay. berries
take their dues in blood
and leave their claws behind.
lay down your denim and leather,
dress yourself in earth's own dye.

flesh of my flesh,
warmed as my flesh by the sun,
bursts in my mouth:
purple juices with clear,
a cinnamon afterglow.
shake the seeds from your hair
and arise, anointed.

the only way to learn which ones to pick
is by picking.

untitled

sunburnt
my skin screams
radiates heat
& cool lotion melts like ice.
it pulls & tears,
reminds me i am alive
& bodily aware.
i soothe, redden, flush,
test, stretch, & stroke,
slip my straps,
turn away a seam
& live inside my skin.

untitled

in my bathroom garbage
pads curl up like caterpillars,
discreetly swathed in tp
which fools no one—
cocoons that never hatch.

rare sister

o rare sister,

accepting our rejection
of the life of suffocated desires and pink curtains
and the life of stereotypes and metal studs.

we stagger
between tradition and anti-tradition,
so embedded in ourselves
that to reject is to die, screaming,
pulling up our own roots;
to accept, a quiet death of avocado carpets,
gold-flecked formica
and ugly orange ashtrays.

with what shall we furnish our lives?
we have no role models;
even feminists get married,
and there are too many cowgirls
to ride off alone into the sunset.

berries

stickery prickery juicy and sweet,
savory berries are yummy to eat.
whether pressed into wine by our bare naked feet
or made into jam and baked in a treat.

just pull out the claws from the blackberry's paws
and smear them all over your face.
then chew each one slow, in your mouth they will go
transporting with each zingy taste.

just give me a berry each day of the week,
bursting with flavor, ripe at its peak.
tarty and tangy, they're not for the meek,
pop each one open with tongue, lips or beak.

blackberry, raspberry, blueberry, more—
better picked wild than bought at the store.
eat all three at once, your taste buds will soar,
chin dribbling wet with runny red gore.

each tiny berry's a world of a treat,
served cold over ice cream or warm brandy heat.
so go find the vines at the end of your street,
stickery prickery juicy and sweet.

untitled

she slides into my bed
at four a.m. always,
the witching hour.

she wraps her arms
around my hips
and presses the soles of my feet
against arizona's red earth.

she shares my pillow,
showing my dreams
how i have not wasted her gifts.

i have made energy from her estrogen
lust from her lh
and peace from her progesterone.

pulling too hard back to center
makes muscles cramp,
but i will stay there for days,
handmaid to her temple,
washing her feet with joy's tears.

winter lamb

when a lamb drops in december
no one expects it
though sheep are made for cold.

wet from the womb, she freezes
to icy blades of grass
moments before
her own warm breath frees her.

her own teats only a forethought,
pressed to cold hard dirt
until her mother's lift her head,
searching like a sunflower.

two wobbly knees, three, four,
standing, the same bitter chill
as when we're first out of the pool.

wool's made for weather
right from the start
as it dries
one snuffling winter's breath at a time.

sweet verse

tercet, octet, sestet, more:
poetry can be such a bore.
forcing rhymes is such a chore:
couplet, quatrain, metaphor.

a terza rima is too terse,
a limerick is too perverse.
now i'm down to choosing "worse"
to have a word that rhymes with verse.

haiku, sonnet, elegy,
save a villanelle for me.
roundel, tanka, prosody,
pantoum, stanza, simile.

cadence, trope and trochaic feet
are things i never cared to meet.
if discipline can make it neat,
tradition sometimes makes it sweet.

facebook haiku week

pumpkin pie, whipped cream
crusty out, soft in, like you,
both spicy and sweet.

my red cheeks, white breath
winter's breeze blows snow to love
your cold nose, warm heart.

typing in text fields,
my whole entire life is
in a pixel box.

breakfast with lizards:
they get beetles; me, coffee—
crunchy and steamy.

wild kingdom moment:
lizard eats beetle; meanwhile,
i hunt coffee beans.

bloody mary 1
pork chops eggs potatoes toast
bloody mary 2

me: messy eater.
peanut butter on my legs,
apples on my lap.

tiny fairy feet
tapping on the windowsill
raindrops commuting

                              shimmying girl fat
                    wibbles under her spandex
                              hot bicycle ride

twenty-six miles, then
fifteen more miles plus dog walk.
can my legs rest now?

                              one warm winter kiss
                    your heat melts my resistance
                              butter thighs soften

squeezing the sponge

my friend anne told me about her theory of creativity many years ago. she said we are like sponges, absorbing everything life has to offer. then eventually we get full and have a creative outburst where our lives and loves flow back out again.

problem was she never specified who or what squeezes the sponge. but i guess that's the big question, isn't it, the one that every artist or writer gets asked. where do you get your ideas? what inspired you? and the question that's just below the surface but that people never ask, how can i get my own sponge squeezed?

sometimes life squeezes us with a beautiful sunset or a touching melody or a warm kiss or a sad movie. but most of the time we are responsible for our own squeezing. writing is hard work and some discipline is required just as the artist must wash out her brushes and put the caps back on her tubes of paint.

most of the time we don't squeeze ourselves. occasionally we have a good reason such as undergoing chemotherapy but mostly the problem lies elsewhere. we're afraid to squeeze our own sponges. there are a lot of things we're afraid of. like it won't be good enough, or it will be too good and we will be expected to continue or to make those difficult sacrifices and compromises that we don't want to make. we are afraid of what others will think of our squeezings or that they'll think we're selfish.

we are afraid that squeezing the sponge will release things that are painful or frightening or unacceptable or disturbing—all qualities of great art.

we want someone else to squeeze our sponges for us. then we can't be blamed if the results come out in a way we don't like. also we're lazy. or we don't think our hands are strong enough. or we don't want to be reminded of the billions of bacteria that grow in our everyday kitchen sponges that don't even die in the microwave and that get smeared over surfaces that touch the food we put into our mouths. so our neuroses get in the way.

and it's true that what gets squeezed out of the sponge isn't always clean...but i would argue that it's always healthy.

the truth is that i can set aside time to squeeze my own sponge any time i want to, i have just convinced myself that i am too busy. well i'm not too busy to breathe or digest, and i need to make this squeezing habit just as natural and transparent. my typewriter's here because i wanted some mechanical assistance today, just as a new staplegun makes you want to go out and tackle some household project. i'm staring at an unfinished one right now, but there's a typewriter between me and the shade cloth. so i guess i'll give this sponge another squeeze.

fallow

fields fall fallow.
we celebrated the harvest already,
you remember,
gorging ourselves on the last of summer's sun.
now it's the lean season.

a chipmunk sees sticks and stems
and knows to pull one nut,
carefully,
for tiny bites.

park ducks rely on human charity.
deer strip trees of bark.
hey, it's horses,
and it's easy to find a mouse
in a haystack now.

wait. rest. slow
to meet your own rhythm, which is hers,
which is the pace of mouse and deer.

grow lean, but full,
on winter's richness.

book of tides

tides turn the pages
of the book this rain is writing
on this beach.

my feet left bookmarks
here yesterday.
i've come this far, thus far.

low tides
task tiny body, small spirit
to fill horizonless sky, water;
i send seagulls to say, sorry.

high tides
lap over a heart
already full; gift, gratitude,
treasures wrapped in foam.

mother nature's tell-all exposé
leaves my soul naked,
my toes cold and wet.

roots

perhaps you've seen the illustration in the science books of the root structure of the tree. still, many people don't realize that there's as much of the tree underground as there is aboveground, if not more: a vast network of roots built to efficiently collect nutrients and water. The largest of these roots, which typically grows straight down, is called the tap root, and in many trees it takes the form of a job, family or relationship.

More roots branch off from the taproot, and more from those, becoming progressively smaller until they take the form of hairs, or cilia. Some cilia are thick enough to see, such as a favorite restaurant or museum, or the sunny bench by a duck pond. Some cilia are so thin that they would break if pulled from the soil, and so we would never see them. These cilia might appear as birdsong in the morning, the smell of sage and creosote after a rain, or how the barista remembers that you drink decaf.

Scientists, working carefully to separate the delicate cilia from the soil, have also observed cilia shaped like a hummingbird's nest in the center court of a shopping mall, a javelina walking on the sidewalk and a cluster of bees that returns each spring to the tree next to the bike path. Just because these cilia are for all practical purposes left in the soil and largely invisible, doesn't mean they're not there.

sex

what he doesn't know

he doesn't know i write at night,
without him.
when he's here, i get fifteen minutes.
when he's gone, it could take all night.

sometimes it's his fantasy,
sometimes mine,
copied from the anthology
and handed over
like a letter to dear abby, saying,

what do you think of this?
it turns me on.

it should. i conceived it,
sometimes with him,
sometimes without, immaculate.
he never knows i start without him, after.
one generative act begets another.

what i didn't do to him this time,
i'll do to him on paper,
then next time, and next.

he never asks, though i answer.
he thinks he wrote the manual on seduction,
but he hasn't read mine, or the lines,
or the sheets, or what lies between.

shared anonymously with strangers,
a dollar a word
buys his breakfast
and my secret satisfaction.

water sign / fire sign

what happens when water meets fire,
feeding the flames?
we get steamy sultry sizzling smoking,
boiling bubbling blasting blazing.

what happens when smoke meets spirit,
intellect drawn through emotion's hookah?
we get sensuousness soaking steeping steaming,
bathing bloody blasphemy breaking breathing.

what happens when leo meets scorpio,
but it's tigers who like to swim?
we get a scorpion on the back of that frog,
drowning itself in its own water sign
with its sharpest sting.
how the hell do you figure that.

what happens when lava meets river,
when vulva meets volcano?
molten stays melted, forever flowing.
when the steam clears,
that's blood on the ground, and tears.

when my thighs meet your bathtub,
your ungrounded spoon
will finish that business once and for all.

my water sign's too hot for me,
my fire sign's too hot for you.
tears freeze at 112 degrees,
floods offer no relief.
in the eternal battle between fire and ice,
there's no winner, but no loser either.

conversations, part ii

if you don't already know
what my knee is saying to your hand,
perhaps you don't need to know.

if you haven't already heard
what your breath said to my breast,
perhaps you should hold it.

if you didn't overhear the gossip
between my hands and your hair,
perhaps i should start a rumor of my own.

if you weren't paying attention
when my hips murmured to your thigh,
perhaps they'll call someone who cares.

if you didn't understand
what your arms said to my waist,
perhaps something was lost in translation.

if you didn't eavesdrop
when my lips whispered to your shoulder,
perhaps you should learn the language.

what you'll do

do you know what i'm going to do to you?
i can't know.

there's what you desire to do to me,
what you're sure you'll do to me,
what you fantasize about doing to me,
what you only idly speculate about doing to me.

there's what you've done to me already,
what you've told me you'll do to me,
what you've promised you'll do to me,
what you've threatened to do to me,
what you threatened not to do to me.

there's what you've never dared to do to me,
what you'd only do to me if,
what you'd only do if no one is watching,
what you'd only do if someone is watching.

there's what you're about to do to me,
what you're starting to do to me,
what you started to do to me then stopped.

there's what i want you to do to me,
what i guess you'll do to me,
what i show you how to do to me.

until you start doing it,
i can't know.

harvest

put your head in the lap of the sun,
grasp the butt of a boulder
and pull yourself into the forest.

curve your leg around a pine tree,
immerse your mouth in the stream,
wet, cold, and sweet.

rub salt between your palms
and softened, stroke seaward.

roll olives between your fingers,
feel fish wiggling through thighs,
press knees tight to branches,
swinging, swinging down.

fruit bursting over buds,
spices scenting skin,
plums, plucked ripely.

what makes you pregnant

these genitals were just
walking down the street
when someone decided
to throw three sheets to the wind,
these sheets to the floor.

short-term planning
is the distance between
the doorway and the bed,
and those are very short shorts indeed.

he flicks away her judgement
by flicking her nipple;
she turns off his control
with her own lack of discipline.

nobody brought the latex, or the forks,
and here's a feast all spread out to consume.
we'll just have to eat with our hands.

body parts are right where they're supposed to be,
just doing what they're supposed to do.
not us.
not i, not you.

discovery channel

his penis slept, soft and sweet
as a kitten in a basket
until her tiger
opened her golden eyes
under cover of brush.
let's see who roars first.

she's one with the sun
till his bite on her neck
sends shock waves down the branch felidae.
let's see what shakes loose.

ah, it was eve in the tree after all,
and now he's grateful for her forked tongue
as she snakes around him.

his trouser salmon
climbs her fish ladder
against all odds
to spawn and be gone.

undone

you think that silk will stop him?
though strong as steel
he'll go right through it, this bull,
to get to your china shop.

he'll unzip your lips
and your hips,
drive through your denim
to your cottony sweet softness.

never cut what can be unbuttoned,
one invitation after another
to the practiced undoing of the heart.

anniversaries of touch

it has been five hours since
we last hugged goodbye,
eight hours since
we slept, spooned, sweetly.

it has been three years since
you last cradled my chin
in your hand,
three weeks since
you last bit my neck.

how can i know
it has been exactly 8 days,
7 hours and 42 minutes since
your fingers were last inside me,
41 days 10 hours and 12 minutes since
you last marked my thigh?

cellular memory both divides and multiplies.
my heart's ticked off the moments
since you last laid palm to pulse.

it's been a lifetime, or only a moment,
but too long.

animal

she sleeps—here—
one eye open, one eye closed
under clothes.

feral aware hair
trigger, uncoiling legs, planting paws
sinking fangs and claws
into flesh fragile and feathery.

licking, pricking, kneading,
needing, she never overthinks.
inhaling the stink
of blood and sweat, nostrils flare,
she's well met.

take her by her scruff, play rough.
she does not brake or break.

be lord over her, or under her be lord,
to be her prey its own reward.

metaphors

i tire of my metaphors.
salt, sea, shells;
orchids and lilies;
rolling hills and mountains and rivers;
with all our universality
can we find no more than flowers?

i would have
the air humid and close with electrical tension,
a crackling, spitting synapse,
a blazing, blinding comet,
a burst of energy, a pull of passion,
the press and slide of arms and arms
and legs and legs.

let us find the firmness of our flesh
in the soft, soft of our poetry.

the same but different

he
takes her in his big strong arms

                        she
              takes him in her big strong thighs

his
mouth is full of her scent

                        her
           mouth is full of words unspoken

he
curls himself into a question behind her

                        she
                       answers it

he
doesn't feel guilty

                        she
         wishes she could but she can't

his
shirt comes down to her knees

                        her
           hair falls down to his knees

he
covers her breasts with his hands

                        she
        covers his eyes with her breasts

he
takes ten minutes

                        she
           comes twice in five

he
puts the room on his credit card

                        she
            gives him credit

he
goes home to his wife

                        she
           goes home to hers.

traveling you

i have wanted to travel you
for some time now,
trace tiny highways, red,
of endlessly cycling cells,
miles of spidery lines reel under my fingers,
cities counties forests valleys
shaded shadowed soft
flesh falling in creases
folded unfolded endless times
like a map.

i straddle both lanes,
unrolling you winding you curving you
under the restless heels
wheels of my hands,
limbs slacken tighten speed and slow to meet
the rising falling terrain.

roll down the window,
let winds of passion lift our clothes,
flatten and tangle our hair
to hopeless masses.
let cruise control remain a factory option—
i will drive.

practice never makes perfect

in our own perfect arrogance
we think we've practiced enough,
but you've never smoothed away
these new hairs from my temple.

these new nails
on the ends of my fingers
have never scratched your back.

you've never soothed this new wrinkle
with a kiss,
nor avoided this new bruise,
and here's a new knot
in an old muscle
that i've never loosened.

this was a place too ticklish to touch.
new neurons formed from new wicked ideas.
if cells renew our selves
every seven years,
then you've never touched me
here, or here, or here.

you've laid your pathways down in my flesh,
mine, in yours.
but oregon falls into the ocean
and oxbows erode,
and mother nature nudges us to higher ground.

joy to build and plant
a new garden every year,
one brick seed cell touch at a time,
practice practice practice.

hot for yourself

you've got to love yourself
before you can love someone else:
excite your own imagination,
fire your own synapses
before you send that heat
through his eyes, her ears,
her core, his cock.

smell your own honest scent
reaching out, reeling in,
primal pheromonic perfume
lighter than air,
subtle as a freight train.

travel your own skin:
every bump in the road,
every scar, every white line.
probe your own wrinkles inside and out,
lubricate your life
with your own juicy self.
catch yourself
in the soft net of your own hair.

squeeze your own arms,
massage your own muscles,
grab giant handfuls of thigh, belly and breast.
find your own hairs and hollows
before anyone else gets lost or falls in.

didn't you practice
kissing your hand as a teenager?
haven't you touched yourself
pretending to be a stranger?

trust me, it isn't like tickling yourself,
to share them sharing you.

see what they see,
feel what they feel,
taste what they taste,
makes it twice as real.

border crossings

you've crossed the border
between sex and lovemaking
so many times that
the border guards now nod and wave you through
without demanding proof of tenderness,
without asking how long you'll stay,
without checking your pockets for condoms.

you enjoy your diplomatic immunity,
don't you.
your drives take you through neighboring countries
countless times, spending a common currency
of caresses and clasps
though the exchange rates fluctuate
from morning to evening
or from bed to couch.

maybe i don't know where you're coming from,
but i know where you've been. souvenirs:
a tiny fetish from a porn film,
dialogue from a french romantic comedy.

i granted you dual citizenship long ago.
i'll eat your regional delicacies
and serve you mine;
i'll wear your folk costume
if you'll learn my word for love.

we'll immigrate, or emigrate,
the ins and outs don't matter,
if you want to go far, go together.

love

incomplete intimacy

the bacon in her fridge
tells me she's a carnivore,
but doesn't say
if she cooks it crispy or soft.

shells on her night stand
show she keeps the ocean close to her heart,
but is it the cold green of the pacific,
the intellectual gray of the atlantic,
or the soft foamy blue of mexico?

her wineglasses say she drinks both red and white,
but does the pinot gris
reflect her taste, or a giver's,
or some specific dish or expectation?

she appears to drink both regular and decaf,
but i, a guest, alter the contents of her icebox
just by opening it,
like shrodinger's cat.

these are incomplete intimacies,
implied knowledge.
sometimes we ask,
but mostly, we connect the dots
of daily life
to draw our own conclusions.

resealable heart

in my lifetime, it took forever
to insert tab a into slot b.
boxes sprouted perforated pour spouts.
soda cans never decided how to open themselves.
can openers will never become extinct.

so when they invented ziploc bags
the world rejoiced.
when the seam turns green, say amen.

in my lifetime, it takes forever
to develop a resealable heart.
one opened too many times
now closes awkwardly, and often.

flaps tear, straps fatigue, snaps snap.
zippers jam, elastic decays,
velcro loses its grip on the world.

best just to leave it open,
lest another button loosen and lose.

receiving end

what have you been saying out loud?
on the other side of the mountains
i can't see your lips
shaping the words
that shape something larger than ourselves.

if naming something makes it real,
have you yet dared name it,
speaking the words
to someone other than yourself?
when a tree fell in the forest, you were there.
and now your best friend's heard all about it.

i have not been on the receiving end
of such magic.
enchantress, not enchanted.
lover, not beloved.
now i'm dragged through a ring of fire,
too close to the teleporter,
assembled one pixel at a time.

your words, witnessed,
take on a life of the mind, and heart.
when it's done making itself real,
i'll stand before it, astounded.

instant soulmate

beware the instant soulmate.
love rarely springs open violently
like a black new york umbrella.

nor should it clutch and snag
at shins and ankles
like some pretty thistle.

time and flesh bind us for a reason.
falling in love
takes at least 32.2 feet per second, per second. look it up.
plumbing the depths of one's soul,
or another's,
takes a lifetime;
there are no shortcuts.
souls mating, without earthly constraints,
takes forever, not microseconds.

the drama of a full-blown rose
commands all our attention,
but it blossomed, quietly, overnight,
when we weren't looking.

we forget that first, roots took hold,
leaves sprouted, buds swelled.

one day we look up and realize
the vine has become one with the house.

faith in pie

he puts his heart in a brownie,
hoping she'll take a first bite
and want another,
nibbling past his crusty edge
to the sweet sensuous fatness
of chips and chunks, nuts
he hopes she'll squirrel away
and not just for winter.

he puts his faith in pie,
hoping the cream tempts her to tartness
so he'll slide over her tongue
and remain forever on her hips.

older and wiser

they're both older and wiser by now.
she's ready for his tricks; so he plays none,
but offers a cup half full,
with a humble request to fill it.

or if he does,
it's to ensnare an assumption
in a logic trap,
or to shepherd an old hurt
past a barbed-wire defense
like some dumb sheep.

she's tensed to flee the shrapnel
of the l-bomb,
eyes rolling, backing like a skittish horse
toward the nearest exit.

so he says it obliquely,
matter-of-factly,
theoretically,
hypothetically,
as though it were happening to someone else,
as though it could happen to anyone.
which it could.
perhaps, even, to her.

she has a thousand reasons why not.
he has only a thousand and one reasons why.

the guest room of the heart

sun streams in
and warms the bed
like any lover.

portraits, paintings
on the walls, books
piled by pillows.

to the casual eye,
someone sleeps here.

guests do,
performing ablutions
in the hallway bath
with the sweet pink fifties tile
and cultured marble counter
they've come to expect,
and therefore never question.

take rest where it's offered.
the duvet is no less downy,
love's lamp's glow no less warm.

trade ya

i'll trade you a night under the stars
for a week under your hands,
and if that's not a fair exchange
i'll hand you a heart
for a piece of your mind,
or trade your tongue for my toes,
your ears for my nose.

i'll see your tent
and raise you silk sheets,
i'll drink your cowboy coffee
if you'll eat my room service.
i'll trade the desire in my hand
for the honest lust in yours,
but your favorite shirt is mine
until i get my robe back.

here's a touch for a tenderness,
a cup of tea for a tidepool.
send me a letter,
i'll send you my scent.
i'll take your crap
if you'll take my attitude
and we'll throw each other the bones later.

any other guy

you say you want to be treated like any other guy.
well there are no special privileges here.
i'll assume your superior physical strength,
and you can carry my load from time to time.

i'll yield to you in the mornings and enjoy it,
but you're not excused from condoms
and it's more work to be on top.

with power comes responsibility:
feel free to move about in the world unharmed,
but you must make it a safe place for me too.

you'll bear the full brunt of my tenderness
and suffer the loss of my cruelty.

equal treatment's both
the promise and the threat
of feminism.
you don't get to pick and choose
between ambivalence and commitment,
frustration and joy,
contempt and respect.
you get the whole nine yards
just like any other guy.

love-ender

the victorians spoke the language of flowers:
poppies for pleasure,
almond for promise,
lavender for devotion,
lilac for first love.

we speak a bastard dialect today;
daisies for innocence,
yellow roses for friendship—
but an iris is now a vulva not a message.

what i need's a bouquet to redirect love:
not to kill it at the root
nor strip it of its leaves,
but to turn adoration into admiration,
obsession into inspiration,
fidelity into exploration.

whose petals won't fan the flames?
whose roots release the soil?

send me not bird's foot for revenge,
nor lobelia for malevolence,
but thistle for nobility
and rue for regret.
the bells of campanula overflow with gratitude.

confuse not lemon with lime,
nor discretion with fornication.
send not thorn-apple when sweetbriar's called for.
better yet, send dandelions,
gone to seed and lighter than air,
dispersing their coquetry elsewhere
with a single sigh.

double and full

this bed is full
in more ways than one
despite its queen blanket
and twin quilt.

they also call a full a double
and if there's room for two
or just for you
then a double is full indeed.

slotted together, spoons in a drawer
never enjoyed this much efficiency.

sometimes this queen
misses her king,
two twin continents away,
crossing a land mass to meet you
in an ocean of cotton,
or down, or whatever's in season.

but when my double is full
and my full is double
my bed is full indeed;
this is all the bed i need.

any woman

it's an embarrassment of riches—
blondes, brunettes and redheads—
and like croesus you can't choose
which gold coin
you're going to put in that slot.

you've hit the jackpot,
but your cup runneth over,
and that coffee & cream
beauty by the jukebox
won't fit in your pocket.

it's full of something else:
your yearning, swelling, groaning desire,
your aching, craving, thirsty need.
any woman will do,
but all of them are not enough.

it's your own fault.
you drew the Five of Cups,
and any woman will fit
in the bed next to you
except the one
who's lying there already.

sweet & salty

you come to me with your heart in your hand,
or is that your cock in your hand?
oh right, you have two hands.

first i see your tree, then your forest.
first you see my ocean, then my waves.

lecherous and loving both begin with an L
and end with a kiss.
raunchy and romantic both begin with I
and end with you.
salty and sweet
are two sides of the same tongue.

moebius solves this neatly, sweetly,
with a band whose two sides are one,
with a strip whose two ends are none.

wings on my back

you saw a woman so carefree and clever,
you saw the worn boots and dusty knapsack;
you thought you could hold me forever and ever,
but you didn't see the wings on my back.

you smiled with my laughter and cried with my tears,
held me under the stars when the sky turned to black,
saw my hopes, my dreams, my love, and my fears,
but you didn't see the wings on my back.

you saw my clear eyes, but they gazed far away;
you saw my possessions all tucked in my pack.
how could you see so much of my heart
but not see the wings on my back?

my spirit was restless, my destiny drawn;
my feet broke your heart as they turned to the path.
you saw what you wanted and loved what you saw,
but you didn't see the wings on my back.

strange fruit

unlike mushrooms from manure
or salt from sand,
fruit
should not be found here
but something is.

who knows what birds drop
in fallow fields; i don't,
but something grows,
strange fruit
out of season
i can't identify
and don't know how to cook.

i am the first human
to eat this new tomato,
smooth flesh yielding to my lips.

i'll sow its seeds
for something even stranger.

a stitch in time

a heart once torn by private grief
now sports a public patch.
the stitches are invisible
but the fabric doesn't match.

kindnesses, accommodations
can't cover edges frayed.
talk, tears, touch, ministrations:
a thousand stitches made.

the life they sewed together
their differences are rending.
unraveled like a sweater,
there's no more hope of mending.

a stitch in time saves nine,
but not this time.

not in mexico

now you are in mexico
and you've left me behind
like an old wrapper,
unable to throw myself into the trash.

pens left without caps,
yard tools left in the rain,
closet doors left open,
a shower that dumps cold water on my head
every time you don't turn off the handle,
which is always.

if that bolt was so important
why did you abandon it
in winter's leaf fall,
far from its companion nut?
nothing holds together now,
metaphorically or literally.

doors closed, without closure,
bang endlessly in the wind,
drafts whistling in my ears,
phantom keys turning in the locks.

while you are in mexico
you cannot unlock them.
you cannot unlock me.

setting the bar

i can cook, clean, sew, fuck, and fix things.
you can cook, clean, shoot, fuck, and fix things.

i like to be naked.
you have a lovely body.
i enjoy my body.
you are unselfconscious.

you like this, what i like.
i like that, what you like.
you serve me coffee in bed.
i serve you breakfast in bed.

you are smarter than i am wicked.
i am tougher than you are loving.
you are braver than i am strong.
i am wiser than you are classy.
you are kinder than i am horny.
i am deeper than you are determined.

i am the unstoppable force,
you are the immovable object.

you are three inches taller than i,
but together we hold the bar level,
and high.

a tree grew

a tree might have grown in brooklyn,
but i grew
away from your wind
like a cypress grows
away from the ocean,
one force of nature
yeilding to the one
that blows the hardest.

i put down roots
but the cliff crumbled into the ocean
and there was nothing
the mermaids could do about that.

i grew leaves,
but my moss never showed north
and your south didn't grow either.

i pined for you.
my cones bore nuts
that fell to ground without a fertile cleft,
salted earth where
you wanted nothing to grow again.

so i packed up my root-bound pot
and took it elsewhere,
my lopsided branches
in dire need of a rag, a pole, a stake
in the future.

now i decide which leaves to pinch,
which leaves to thrive;
when to throw in the towel,
when to pick up a trowel.

a lake of a watering pot
fills a hole the size of the earth,
the sun my grow lamp,
the birds my witnesses.

hummer

i don't understand why you come around now.
my windchimes have been calling your name for months,
pot metal shaped like hummingbirds,
one fake weighs more than two real.

you can't be seeking
this clanging, metallic mockery
of your own species' gentle murmur.

nothing blooms here
but flowered towels on the line.
there's no red in the yard
but my passion
and my lopper pole.

perhaps you follow the bees;
you both buzz.
i stopped singing in the shower
but maybe you heard me hum over dishes.

does my pollen intoxicate you?
i'm germinating too.
come sip from my feeder.
i've made it sweet for you.

flesh from flesh

this wishbone is already broken,
this quick merciful death already past.
now all that remains
is to separate flesh from flesh.

my bones haven't grown since we met;
there's not enough marrow
to transfuse two.

now to separate flesh from heart,
that takes hard work
and a good therapist.

stripped of my old skin,
nerves raw,
i succeed too well
in covering myself
in fat that melts only slowly
from rekindled appetites
for more flesh,
not your flesh.

i'll slake my thirst
with my own blood.

www.ingramcontent.com/pod-product-compliance
Lightning Source LLC
Chambersburg PA
CBHW020516030426
42337CB00011B/409